Thoughts at Midnight

AF632691

Renae Smith

BookLeaf Publishing

Presentation by *BookLeaf Publishing*

Web: www.bookleafpub.com

E-mail: info@bookleafpub.com

ISBN: 9789357213202

First edition 2023

Astronomer

You gaped at me
Like you were an astronomer
Discovering the stars

You searched me
Like you were forming constellations
From my heart

You claimed you loved me
Because of the patterns
That you fabricated

But were you actually in love with me
Or with these expectations of me?

Pieces

You're in search of yourself
But you're lost

You venture through sleeping pills,
Empty vodka bottles,
Hoping it glues what is left of you together
But it only erodes it

They broke you
And you gave them the pieces

You gather the crumbs of yourself
But it will never make you whole
Because you give away
Any sliver of yourself you gain again

Content

I hope there are days when you wake up and you don't hesitate to get out of bed. The smiles you give are true, and they are uplifting to witness. I hope you are so energized that you forget to order your coffee. I hope you feel so content and secure with yourself that you forget to pick at your fingernails. I hope you listen to your music and never skip a song because each one touches your heart. I hope you pet the cutest dog on your way to work, and buy flowers for yourself on the way home because you know you deserve them. I hope you open your windows to catch the rays of the setting sun before it disappears for the night. I hope that as you lie down to rest, you remember these little moments for the days that are hard to get out of bed.

Striking Matches

Our love was a flame

And I'm glad I blew it out

Self Taught

As these tears
Turn to flames
I tell myself
I'll be okay
You were always
The one to blame
For these years
Dealt with pain
And now my thoughts
Aren't insecure
They mean nothing
Anymore
For you have shown
That you don't care
So why should I
If you're not here?

Insomnia

Stay up with me

Let me ask you random things
That you might find odd
But that matter to me

Let me trace stars on your skin
And tell you stories of a life
I have yet to live

Let me look at you
At the indescribably
Perfect person you are

Let me listen to your heart
As your breath slows
And your eyes shut

Let me fall asleep here
Because I can't sleep
Without your warmth

Soar

"Why is falling in love scary?" the little girl asked her mom.

"Well," she began. "Think about what it means to be brave. Picture two men with fragile wings, standing on top of a windy cliff. One man is timid and doesn't dare look out onto the view. He is afraid to be reminded of the height he stands at. The other looks out with hope and determination. The first man had never gone up this high and had never been close to feeling the pain of hitting the ground. But the second man had grown used to the heights. He adored them each time he traveled up there; his only fear was never being able to climb to the top again. The first man yells at the second man 'Step back! It's dangerous!' But the second man calls back to him 'It's beautiful.' Reluctantly, the first man says 'We're too high above the ground!' The second man calmly replies. 'Only closer to the heavens.' The first man, still worried, shouts again. 'But you could fall!' The second man pauses and closes his eyes. Then he says 'or I could soar', and jumps off the cliff. You see, falling in love is scary and it's risky. There will be times where you will fall, and it will hurt you in the end. You will fall from different heights, break many bones, and gain new bruises each time you do. But you can't give up. Somewhere there is someone who will provide you with enough wind that will sustain your flight. And you will begin to soar. You will spread your wings so wide that you won't even see the tips of them. And if there are moments you feel you are about to fall, don't let it overwhelm you. The turbulence is nothing compared to what is in store for you. Touch the clouds with your fingertips. Breathe in the frigid air. Feel the wind caress your skin. And finally, at the end of your journey, you will reach peace. You can gently rest your aching wings and look back with nostalgia and pride. You will see others who didn't have as much courage as you did to jump. It might dishearten you, but don't let it take away the flame in your heart."

Inescapable

My mind is a house
With walls
Covered in words and thoughts.
My least favorite room
Is one you've visited
Frequently.
It is an empty room
But it has every
Nasty,
Spiteful,
Inhumane name
I've ever been called
Carved into its walls
Permanently.

Drunk

Late nights
Deafening music
Silhouettes
Intoxicating

Thunderstorms
Grey skies
Blurry vision
Long drives

Our relationship was a haze
And I was drunk in love

But I sobered up

Enlighten Me

I find myself thinking of questions I would love to ask you if only I had the courage. Like, what is the most astonishing place you've ever seen? And, what is your favorite instrument? Tell me about the person who takes your breath away. And the person you feel most comfortable talking to. Where is your safe place? What is something humanly impossible that you dream of doing? If you could paint your thoughts, what would it look like? What would be the theme song of your life? Where would you go if you could go anywhere right now? And what does love mean to you?

Losing You

I have you
But you are water
Slipping through my fingers

Ocean

The ocean in your eyes swallows me whole but I don't want to surface. It is warm and rich and comforting. This passion fills my heart and floods my veins until it becomes part of me. Your name stains my world like ink on paper, and my mind floats through faint thoughts of you. Even the most powerful current couldn't keep from you.

Writing

The words I need
Already surround me
But I can’t form a single sentence.
My thoughts are suffocating
As they try to
Organize themselves.
I hope this poetry
That has been building up in me
Bleeds onto the paper
And sticks

Cleaning

It’s okay to be a mess. Being a mess means you’re unorganized, but that’s because you are organizing yourself and organizing can be messy even though you’re organizing.

Snow

I long for warm weather
And sunshine
And sandy beaches
But
There is something
Incomparably
Infatuating
About the way
Snow kisses the ground.
It makes me think of you
And the way you
Smiled at me
As it floated
Around your face
And clung to your hair.
Your hands were so warm
And your breath heated the sky
Despite the frigid air
And the blanket of frost
Around us

Fear

You've barricaded your heart
To protect it
From hurting again.
But you cannot
Shield yourself with fear
Without detriment.
Your mind is weary
And your heart is collecting dust
From the time spent
Away from the sun.

Stay

I wish the sun wouldn't go
Because you'll have to go too
And I'm tired of being lonely
At midnight

In My Head

I find comfort in my solitude.
I am free to wander
Deep into the caves
Of my thoughts.
I fall in love with
Every pattern
The cracks make on the walls
And every echo
Calling back to me.
I like to admire
The winding of the passages
That venture into my head.
The farther I walk,
The more I discover.
The more I discover,
The more confident I feel
About myself.

It Was Always You

You wrote me paragraphs
I wrote you novels

You murmured lyrics
I sang albums

You sailed rivers
I traveled oceans

You ignored me
I noticed you

You tolerated me
I adored you

You declared our future
I promised it

You broke me
I healed you

You added me to your life
But I dedicated you to the rest of mine

You left
But I stayed

Razor

I was sharp when we first met. You were cautious. You had to be careful using me so I wouldn't hurt you. But the more you did, the more comfortable with you I became. I was one of the many objects you used daily, and I was beneficial to you because I was only ever taught to give. Not to ask or to take, but to benefit as many people as I can for as long as I can. My blades became dull. I was so dependent on you for my own satisfaction that I lost myself in the process of helping you. My one and only purpose failed you so you disposed of me. I questioned everything about myself and why I wasn't capable of earning your loyalty although I wasn't to blame. I wasted so much time trying to fix myself to be deserving of your attention, though I deserved better than you. But the only way to fully recover was to save myself.

Ignorant

Your arrogance deafens you.
I scream at the top of my lungs
But you don't hear me.
You mute the idea of messing up
Because you are incapable of doing so
Even though there are piles of messes
Following behind you.

www.ingramcontent.com/pod-product-compliance
Lightning Source LLC
Chambersburg PA
CBHW051722130826
49812CB00034B/1302
* 9 7 8 9 3 5 7 2 1 3 2 0 2 *